WALL STREET

WOMAN

═══A DATING LIFE═══

By Lisa Padrona and P. Joan Kent
Illustrations by Wanda Shigenaga

An Official
Vice Presidents Anonymous

VICE PRESIDENTS
🚫 5:00
9:00
ANONYMOUS

Publication

Visit our website at www.StillwaterPress.com for more information.

First Stillwater River Publications Edition

Library of Congress Control Number: 2018943235

ISBN-13: 978-1-946-30056-0
ISBN-10: 1-946-30056-x

1 2 3 4 5 6 7 8 9 10

Written by Lisa Padrona and P. Joan Kent
Illustrated by Wanda Shigenaga
Published by Stillwater River Publications, Pawtucket, RI, USA.

Publisher's Cataloging-In-Publication Data
(Prepared by The Donohue Group, Inc.)

Names: Padrona, Lisa. | Kent, P. Joan. | Shigenaga, Wanda, illustrator.
Title: Wall Street woman : a dating life / by Lisa Padrona and P. Joan Kent ; illustrated by Wanda Shigenaga.
Description: First Stillwater River Publications edition. | Pawtucket, RI, USA : Stillwater River Publications, [2018] | "Vice Presidents Anonymous."
Identifiers: ISBN 9781946300560 | ISBN 194630056X
Subjects: LCSH: Dating (Social customs)--New York (State)--New York--Humor. | Securities industry--United States--Employees--Humor. | Brokers--New York (State)--New York--Humor. | Wall Street (New York, N.Y.)--Humor. | Satire, American. | LCGFT: Humor.
Classification: LCC PN6231.D3 P34 2018 | DDC 818.602--dc23

The views and opinions expressed in this book are solely those of the authors and do not necessarily reflect the views and opinions of the publisher.

Contents

THREE MONTHS after I graduated from an elite women's college, magna cum laude in economics, I started the management training program of a major multinational financial corporation in New York.

I was 22.

This is what happened.

JACK OF HEARTS

How He Expresses His Interests

"I can do twice as many laps when I'm sober."

How He Presents His Accomplishments

"Did I go to prep school? I went to four of 'em. In 3 years. I got expelled from the last two. Why? How the hell do I know?"

"So my boss, William Pennington Fathead, said that my talents were better suited to another vocation. So I told William Pennington Fathead that he could shove his iPhone up his ass. So I got fired instead."

How He Tells You He Likes You

"Until you arrived, this party was booooorrrrrrring!"

"Those are the sexiest damn glasses I've ever seen!"

"You're the most tastefully dressed woman I've ever met!"

"Tell me about yourself. You must be interesting."

"You're so damned beautiful. I don't know what to do with myself. Where have you been all my life?"

"I'm berserk over big women! So much to love!"

"We were made for each other."

How He Asks You to Bed

"I live right around here somewhere."

How He Talks About Your Future Together

"Jesus! We've got to get out of here! I have to get to work!...Whatever the hell that is."

"You're such a sweet girl. And I'm such a fuckup. I'm going out right now to drown my sorrows."

"I'm not here."

Why You Should Date Him

You want to be somebody's goddess for at least 5 minutes.

You want a floorshow with dinner.

You need 10 continuous hours of sex and debauchery.

BOY WONDER

How He Expresses His Interests

"God, if you didn't see Wisconsin whip Kentucky in the NCAA semi-final you haven't seen basketball."

How He Presents His Accomplishments

"Everyone thought ARFX would go to 130. But not me! When it hit 125 I sold it short and, guess what? It dropped to 110! Big bucks for the smart boy from Cincinnati."

"I'm not big on cabs. And who really needs Gucci, the Palm or Morimoto? My Berkshire Hathaway stock was bought with the money I saved by eating at home."

"This bicep? Unnh! Last year: 12 inches. This year: 13!"

How He Tells You He Likes You

"I feel I can relax with you. Be myself."

"I need a woman who will be strong when I am weak. Who will make me feel free. You make me feel free."

"You're beautiful."

How He Asks You to Bed

"This is the perfect two-person basketball watching couch. Music. We don't have to watch basketball."

"I find your tenderness and maternal instincts to be very attractive things in a woman. I really respect that."

"You seem tense. Let me massage your shoulders."

How He Talks About Your Future Together

"Guess what? I'm going to be best man at my younger brother's wedding. He's only 28. How can he be ready?"

"I realized my last girlfriend wasn't right for me when she made a big scene at Ray's Pizza. She thought I wanted to live with her. I find this out at Ray's?"

"Three years is not enough time to know if we are right for each other."

"I've always wanted a woman who could tell when I needed to be alone."

"It's my fault. It really is. I'm nothing but trouble and I don't want to hurt you. But I don't want to lose touch. Maybe when I get my act together we could have drinks."

Why You Should Date Him

You want to learn more about spectator sports.

You want to save money.

You need help improving your figure.

You need an escort for business events who can talk about things that really interest your colleagues and customers.

BORN AGAIN BACHELOR

How He Expresses His Interests

"Tension is being stuck in the subway when your date is waiting uptown in bed."

How He Presents His Accomplishments

"I've been out every night this week. It's hot shit."

"I got a new waterbed in my apartment. I got a catamaran in Amagansett. I got a Porsche Carrera. You can see all three in just under 90 minutes."

"I like scuba diving. You ever dive naked?"

How He Tells You He Likes You

"The markets are crazy." (He pats your knee.)

"I think it will snow tomorrow." (He grasps your arm.)

"You don't feel fat." (He runs his fingers down your spine.)

How He Asks You to Bed

"Let's go to my place and get it on."

How He Talks About Your Future Together

"My last date was half my age. Right out of Hustler. But she couldn't understand me. Don't know why."

"My ex-wife took me to the cleaners."

"I'm going to spend the rest of my life on booze, broads and motels."

How He Says Goodbye

"It's not your fault. I probably drank too much."

"Don't you have to work today?"

"Keep your sense of humor. Women my age are so bitter."

Why You Should Date Him

You are convinced that every man you meet will reject you.

You need someone harmless and entirely predictable with no strings attached.

You need proof that marriage doesn't always result in perpetual bliss.

DIALTONE

Have you ever met a man and not realized it?

How He Expresses His Interests

"I have brunch on Sundays with my roommate."

"I make hamburgers for dinner every night."

"I go to the movies sometimes."

When you pursued any of the interests he divulged, did you find yourself in a conversation like:

"Have you thought of making chicken instead of hamburgers?"

"Can't."

"Why not?"

"Takes too long."

"How about roast beef?"

"I burned it last time."

"I've got a good recipe for filet of sole in dijonnaise sauce..."

"Too complicated."

"How about Chef's Salad?"

"Don't like carrots. Don't like tomatoes. Don't like celery."

"Have you tried regular salad?"

"Lettuce turns brown in the refrigerator."

"What about potatoes?"

"I had a bag of them once. They grew pods. I can keep hamburger in the freezer. It doesn't rot."

How He Presents His Accomplishments

"I majored in psychology."

'I've seen every re-run of Law and Order."

"I'm a CPA. It's really interesting."

How He Tells You He Likes You

"I thought you looked familiar."

"Where did you go to college?"

"Do you come to these parties often?"

"What was your major?"

"Do you own or rent your apartment?"

How He Asks You to Bed

"I guess you don't want to come up for a cup of coffee."

How He Talks About Your Future Together

"I guess you want to see other men."

Why You Should Date Him

Your doctor tells you to get some rest because of high blood pressure.

You don't want to go to the movies alone, and you don't want to talk, touch, or think about your date during the feature.

You want to date someone who definitely doesn't have an STD.

CLOUD VOYAGER

How He Expresses His Interests

"Could we head over to the Native American Center? There is a performance of Apache war chants at 8. Good prep for my trip to Santa Fe."

"I never fully recovered from that bout of tapeworm. You'd think that at 33 I'd know better than to eat barbecue in Burkina Faso."

"Am I too short to be a bullfighter?"

How He Presents His Accomplishments

"This scar was made by a Pygmy spear. I was investigating their fertility rites for my master's thesis, and I got caught up in the wrong rite."

"I lost my Navy dress sword in Cochabamba during the annual Bolivian coup. I sliced at what I thought was a rebel lieutenant but—it was some sort of mango tree."

"My Gila monster has dual citizenship."

How He Tells You He Likes You

"You could have been Nefertiti in your last life."

"Let's go to Tierra del Fuego tonight."

"My duck likes you."

How He Asks You to Bed

"Hi. This is Sir Lancelot. I'm outside. I figured that you'd still be awake [it's 3a.m.]. We can bake cookies or something."

How He Talks About Your Future Together

"I almost got married in grad school. But her parents objected—she was a Kazakh princess, after all. Last I heard, she was running guns to Zimbabwe. I don't think that I'll be lucky enough to find another woman who is so simpatica."

"Oh, that? That's my visa application for the Sheik Hamid Bank and Trust. I'm off for a stint in Riyadh."

"If you're ever in Phnom Penh...."

Why You Should Date Him

You don't have time to both date and watch the Travel Channel.

You want help reading menus in Urdu and Albanian.

You've never spent a night in an apartment with Zambesi weapons, Kabuki masks, medieval armor, a barber chair, and a duck that quacks in Welsh and Lao.

Your last date was with Dialtone.

DON JUAN DINERO

Have you ever met a man whose every word and gesture leaves you weak with desire?

How He Expresses His Interests

"Ciao, Carissima! Come stai? How pleasant to see you here. Only one day and already so long!... May I present Signora Pippa Middleton?"

"Could your secretary call Nobu for me? Gracias... I think I forgot my wallet there last night... But if not, perhaps Bobby De Niro took it home for me. Could she call him too?"

How He Expresses His Interests

"My boss tells me to remain en oficina while he takes holiday next week. But I have invited some friends to Gstaad and it's too late to change. He's an idiot. Americans are too serious. Can you come to Gstaad tonight? All you must bring is a toothbrush. I can buy everything else."

How He Presents His Accomplishments

"I do not work at the bank now. I want to understand the real estate market in this country before I leave. So I will work for some time with Manifest Land Organization. Are you familiar with real estate, Bambina?"

"I do not work with Manifest Land right now. I want to understand commodity markets in this country before I leave. So, I will work with Berndt Von Ludendorff at Grainco. He is a friend of the family. Have you ever dealt with commodities, Cara Mia?"

"I do not work at Grainco anymore. I want to understand the stock market in this country before I leave.
So I will work for some time with Goldman Sachs. My
cousin Dmitri from Zurich is a Director. What do you
think of stocks, Ma Bella Donna?"

"I do not work at Goldman Sachs anymore. My merger
was interrupted by Grand Cinzano Regatta. Of course,
you know it? Newport to New Guinea and back. Yes. I
had to navigate my own ship. I couldn't let anyone
else do it this time! You will crew for me next year.
No? I shall be ecstatic."

How He Tells You He Likes You

"Bongiorno, Bellisima!"

"When I look up from my desk each day and see you
have left for the subway, I am devastated."

"These flowers were the last ones they had at the
shop. Someone had ordered them for a funeral. I told
them the flowers were for a beautiful woman, not for
a funeral. I told them I wanted the flowers. I told them
I would buy the shop if they didn't give me the flowers. And yet the flowers are nothing compared to
you."

"Your eyes make me wild with desire!"

"You teach the torches to burn bright."

How He Asks You to Bed

"In my country, a man isn't a man unless he has a mistress."

"You American women need real men."

"After the Ball, you must come to my penthouse. All you have to bring is a toothbrush. I can arrange everything else."

"I will make you scream in ecstasy and crawl up the walls."

How He Talks About Your Future Together

"Of course, Amore, I want to be with you again. Soon. But I must go home to Bogota for a few months. I must manage the family companies while my father travels in Luxembourg."

"One of my younger sisters will live with me in New York. Of course, I must be her chaperone. I will not have much time for you, Carissima. My heart is heavy!"

"My business will keep me in Montevideo for some months. So unfortunate! I have no words for my sorrow."

"I shall languish far from the oceans of your eyes."

Why You Should Date Him

There are excellent reasons to date Don Juan Dinero:

You want to meet George Clooney, Renzo Piano, Salman Rushdie, Mark Zuckerberg, Oprah Winfrey, and Prince Harry.

You've never attended a rock concert on a private Dreamliner.

You want to go to the latest ultimate club before the stringers from Vanity Fair, New York, and Rolling Stone discover it.

You won't want to wait in line at the latest ultimate club.

You don't want to wait in line anywhere.

You want to scream in ecstasy and crawl up the walls.

CLUB CADET

How He Expresses His Interests

"I had food poisoning once. I ate at an Ethiopian restaurant in Little Italy—never do that again! I had to miss Elon Musk's speech at the University Club.

"That's the last time I wear black tie below 50th Street."

"I think Tokeneke is among the finest country clubs on the East Coast. I was a bartender there for several summers. Great people. Loved 'em."

How He Presents His Accomplishments

"I thought of going to Harvard, but I really preferred Colby. So I went there instead. I wouldn't be where I am today if I'd spent my undergrad days at the 'Vard."

"Corporate Finance at Morgan Stanley would be a good fit for my credentials, but then again it's just selling things. Anyone from Queens can sell things."

"I won't be taking a vacation this summer since I plan to spend all my weekends in the Hamptons. It's the same house I shared last year. Very relaxed. I don't have to do what everyone else is doing, and it's a great crowd. A junior editor from Town and Country lives next door."

How He Tells You He Likes You

"What nationality is your name?"

"Does your father enjoy his business?"

"You mean you know girls who went to Vanderbilt? That's great! The best! Betsy, Freddie, Missy, Puffy, and Veronica went there and they're super."

"Oh, hi. The reason I phoned was to see if you'd like to go to the City Ballet benefit tonight. Without thinking, I bought two tickets instead of one and I know you like dance. We could have dinner beforehand or better yet we could just meet there and have some hors d'oeuvres and drinks."

"Are you a cross-country skier? I'm driving a group of friends up to Lake Placid this weekend in my BMW. One of my contacts has a hut with a fireplace, a Jacuzzi, and 10 cases of Heineken. There's room in the car if you'd like to join us."

How He Asks You to Bed

He never will. He'll just create a situation where there is no other option. Then he'll get drunk.

It will be at a toga party or a group skinny dip in the Hamptons where everyone else is attempting to get into bed too. You'll know he wants to make love when he stumbles over and says, "Hey, there's this great judo trick a friend of mine showed me in prep school. Wanna try it?"

If you're alone in his apartment, he'll say, "I know the Barleys who own Topsiders II. They developed this terrific drink called a 'stumplifter.' I've made a pitcher. They're good friends of mine."

When he falls asleep on your bed, it's time to make love.

How He Talks About Your Future Together

The Club Cadet doesn't date a woman who isn't a potential girlfriend, and she can't be a girlfriend unless she's a potential wife. Otherwise it wouldn't look good. If he invites you out, you've clearly got potential.

However, it is very easy to trip one of his social land mines—like spilling food on your blouse at the country club, or arriving in a cocktail-length dress when the other women are wearing evening gowns. He'll drop you. If he didn't, it would look bad.

After that happens the next thing you'll hear is: "I know a guy at work who isn't going out with anyone. You and he have the same—you know—background, so you should have a lot in common."

Why You Should Date Him

You'll get to meet a bunch of guys from his office. Guys who are ethnic or from the Midwest. You might find one who is interesting.

HOPALONG HUSBAND

How He Expresses His Interests

"This division has the best performance in the company because I built it that way. You can be part of its success. But you'll have to be very attentive to what I say, and follow me closely."

"Sometime we'll have to sit down and talk stock market strategy. I'm very curious to see what you can bring to the table."

How He Presents His Accomplishments

"I've restructured this organization along matrix lines to improve cross-selling and efficiency. It's funny; you and I don't need a matrix to communicate."

"My little Sally is so precocious. She sewed all the buttons on my raincoat. Only 7 years old. She's beautiful. Just like you."

"Doris and I have grown apart. She doesn't understand me. Unlike you."

How He Tells You He Likes You

"Why not consider a married man? Women complain about the lack of acceptable single men. Well, that's because the best ones are taken."

"My wife and I have an open marriage. We know it's unrealistic to think that others won't turn us on."

"You wouldn't by any chance want to go to Jazz at Lincoln Center? We're taking some customers and Doris can't make it."

How He Asks You to Bed

"OK. I admit it. I'm drunk. And I admit you're drunk. But why not? You're the toast of Chicago. Everyone loved your presentation. You did great…. Oops, I'll help you to your room. Wouldn't want you to fall into the pool. Ooops, you just dropped your key. Here, I'll open the door."

"I love you."

"We should be like this forever."

How He Talks About Your Future Together

"I can't. I simply can't. No matter how much—God—I want to. You can't know what this does to me. But I can't. For the kids' sake."

"We simply can't go on. For your sake. It's not fair to you."

"I've talked to J.B. He feels that you've made so much progress that you're ready for a promotion. He thinks that you can handle the Houston office."

Why You Should Date Him

You want to be told that you're the most ravishing woman in the world.

You'd like a relationship but want to reserve your weekends and holidays for things that really interest you, like tennis, Bermuda, and tap dancing lessons.

THE VISIONARY

Ever wonder what it would be like to date one of those guys who gets grants from your corporate Support of the Arts Division?

How He Expresses His Interests

"Da Vinci, Velazquez, Rembrandt. Representational Art. Bourgeois, trite, meaningless, dead—they shouldn't be seen in museums. They should be hung at the end of the aisles in large grocery stores."

"True Art is how you think about the canvas. Not about what's on it. What's on it is just magic tricks, like the kind you see at the circus."

"Nothing is what it seems. If you want Truth, paint Nothing."

How He Presents His Accomplishments

"The art market is a closed capitalist society built by the rich on the backs of the poor, and filled with bureaucrats, pinheads, and Art Appreciation majors from Wellesley and Duke."

"I reject their rejections. I burn their critiques at 38th and Madison. Yes, every year. During the Vernal Equinox."

How He Tells You He Likes You

"Come over tonight some time. I'm stretching canvas. I'm listening to Mahler. You were made for Mahler."

How He Asks You to Bed

"Mahler's 7th is deeply sensual. It's all about ecstasy. The ecstasy of despair."

"You are profoundly sensual. Surely you've posed before. Nude."

"Of course it doesn't look like you! I don't paint the naked body as it is. Art is about the sensation—the Gestalt! That's what you are looking at on the canvas—The Gestalt!"

How He Talks About Your Future Together

"Listen, tonight I'm going over to Puffy's. Jeff Koons is supposed to show up. So why don't I see you tomorrow night?"

"The only thing created by commitment in the last 50 years is suburbia. I can't paint in Paramus."

Why You Should Date Him

The Visionary is the ideal candidate for those times when:

You're afraid you've lost touch with what's going on outside work.

You want to wear a sarong when you go out for dinner.

You want to meet men who don't know what stocks, bonds, and putting greens are.

You want to see and discuss some of those erotic political movies from Eastern Europe.

TREADMILL

How He Expresses His Interests

"I work shorter hours during the summer. I usually leave the office before 9 p.m., when they turn off the air conditioning."

"Just bought a satellite charger for my smartphones and laptops. Can't risk a power outage if there's another hurricane."

"The office is nice and quiet when I get in at 7 a.m. And I beat the breakfast rush in the cafeteria."

How He Presents His Accomplishments

"Company stock was up six bucks today. That's good news for my options."

"I cut back my deck to 38 slides. But I was still able to make all the mission-critical points to the chairman."

"I've lived in three cities in 7 years. You just can't say no when they ask you to fix a problem subsidiary. You can't let the company down."

How He Tells You He Likes You

"I ordered dinner for my team from Charlie's down the street so we can finish the budget tonight. I brought you a slice."

How He Asks You to Bed

"You really have a head for business. Let's grab drinks at Charlie's across the street. I can show you my department's projections."

"I have a studio near the office so I can put in the hours. In fact, my place is only a few blocks away. That's where I left the projections."

How He Talks About Your Future Together

"You'll have to go home before midnight. I've got a conference call then with Tokyo."

"I'm being transferred to Buenos Aires. We need more seasoned leadership there."

Why You Should Date Him

You'll see him at the office. Your dates will be drinks or dinner near the office. At Charlie's, for example. You'll stay over in his apartment near the office. What could be simpler or more geographically convenient? And not at all expensive—you have to dress nicely anyway when you go to work so you don't need separate date clothes. Treadmill won't cheat on you, except, perhaps, with his wife—the woman he never talks about.

But not to worry too much. It's a good bet she sleeps in a separate room when he's there, so she won't be awakened by conference calls in the night.

The only woman Treadmill will spend any of his scarce time with is a woman who works where he works. Since HQ isn't big enough for him to carry on with more than one at a time, that means you're it!

After a while, Treadmill will be re-assigned to a foreign division. This saves you the trouble of breaking up with him when it gets just way too dreary.

MAJOR GELATIN

Have you ever dated a man who is perfect in every way except that he's married?

THE CHARING CROSS

How He Expresses His Interests

"I'm embarrassed when I remember my Hasty Pudding costumes. I'm sure they are still at Harvard in some basement somewhere. I pray every day they don't find the videos!"

"Walden Pond is a knock out. I just re-read it over the weekend at our place in Maine."

"Sailing is existential. You go from one place to another with the wind. And from this century to another one."

How He Presents His Accomplishments

"Wish I hadn't been profiled in the Journal. Everyone's asking for money. Even my 10-year-old."

"If we top the deal list this year, they'll bump me up a notch. I'm taking the whole team up the ranks with me."

"I've doubled my grandfather's portfolio. Conservative, value-investing, but now it's diversified."

"My wife doesn't really know what I do. I wish she did."

How He Tells You He Likes You

"Remember me? We met 6 months ago at the negotiations on the Mega Tilt merger."

"Sorry if I was staring at you. I was trying to remember how long it's been since we bumped into each other."

"Four months! Couldn't have been."

"It was great working against you on Mega Tilt. You did a really great job for them—Everyone saw what you did. I think a lot about it, and a lot about you."

"What a surprise to see you downtown... Yes, I was recruited away from Stoughton and Pickering a few months ago. Now with Cabot, Perkins and Lowell. Number 1 Wall Street. Delmonico's is my favorite haunt at happy hour. I'm here all the time."

"Doing anything Saturday afternoon, before six?"

"Great! Meet me at the 79th Street Boat basin. I'll take you out on a sail—the Charing Cross—up to the Catskills and back."

How He Asks You to Bed

"You know, I was beginning to think it would never happen. I'm finding out now what having a soulmate means."

"You don't know how you've affected me."

"Are you feeling what I'm feeling?"

"I haven't been touched lovingly by a woman in years. No. Actually—ever."

"I'm sure I was in love with her when we married. But I had no idea what love truly was."

"I bought a new Land Rover. Just for us. The keys are at the garage. Two sets of keys. I've got a parking space there just for us too."

"Here's to us. To us, the Charing Cross, rosy-fingered dawn, and the wine-dark sea."

"Have another glass. If you get tired, I have the key to a suite upstairs."

How He Talks About Your Future Together

"My wife spends her weekends cruising the streets of New York. She saves stray cats. It's a charity."

"There is cat urine all over the Queen Anne furniture."

"She's on Nantucket for all of August. She's taking the kids."

"Save August."

"Open the envelope. Two round-trip tickets to St. Barts."

"Alright, finally, it's done. I'm getting a divorce. I started Barnaby assembling the papers today."

"My God! She's found out about us!"

"She's filed papers! She's going to take everything! The cottage, Linden Hall, Wendover Farm, Nantucket and the Colony. Charing Cross. She's even taking the kids."

"Dearest, my darling—Barnaby says we can't be seen together."

"Ever again. Never ever again!!!"

"It would kill me in court."

"But I meant everything I said! Darling, dearest, my soul! I love you! I will love you forever!!"

Why You Should Date Him

How often do you get to go out with a traditional Ivy League guy who has it all—the boat, the brains, the ancestors, the bank account, the great lawns, good taste, tickets to the opera, and a career extolled by the Wall Street Journal? And he loves you for your brains and talent as well as everything else? Yes, he has everything you need to become a dynasty. And you deserve him because he's perfect. Except that he has a wife who will take it all away.

It's a problem.

He's slow on the draw. When he draws, he doesn't pull the trigger. Then when the bullets start flying, he breaks for the exit. At warp speed.

But look at the bright side. You are his soul mate. He still loves you. You can't have each other. It's romantic. Now, Voyager.

And it's not a total defeat. If you've dated Gelatin, you've reached the top of the social heap. Which means you're good enough to date all the guys who believe that Gelatin is better than them; people like Club Cadet and Boy Wonder.

In case you really want to go out.

TEEN CRUSH (THEN)

How He Expresses His Interests

"Healthcare administration is full of challenges. Everyone's different and procedures are changing all the time. You've got to keep up."

"The work at the Mira Loma Street clinic keeps me busy even on slow days."

"I love living in Chico. It's been a great place to raise my kids."

"My ex-wife—you remember Becky?—lives across the street from my new apartment. Makes joint custody so much easier."

"Paul—you remember him?—football?—talked me into a fly fishing trip. Can't wait."

How He Presents His Accomplishments

"Yeah—I played football at State. But just freshman year. It took up way too much time."

"I was relieved when I got laid off at Memorial. Being the assistant administrator was prestigious, but it was very disorganized—full of conflict. Not that managing a doctor's office is exactly relaxing."

"I just applied for my first passport. Taking the kids to Vancouver in August."

How He Tells You He Likes You

"This convention is doing a good job of presenting IT issues in healthcare. It was why I wanted to come here to New York... well, one of the reasons."

"Do you still have our prom pictures? I'd like to make copies."

"I was so proud to go with you. It was unforgettable."

"Remember Place d'Etoile Night?—Never again!"

"... and then Mr. Long did the locker search."

"And Miss Sharp got fired for reading that part from Huckleberry Finn."

"How often do you get back home to Chico?"

How He Asks You to Bed

"When you visit Chico, you don't have to stay with your parents."

How He Talks About Your Future Together

"Many people from our class are still in town. You'd be surrounded by friends."

"San Bartolomeo still has weekly bingo. It's fun to go with the kids. And of course there is the spaghetti dinner."

"There must be lots of job opportunities in Chico for someone with your knowledge of finance."

"My apartment is in that new Tropicana complex—the one just two blocks west of your mom and dad's."

"Becky and the kids have keys to my place."

How He Says Goodbye

"I lived in the big city once. Summer internship in Sacramento. It just isn't for me."

Why You Should Date Him

Those times when everything is going wrong, you feel terrible about yourself and your career, and you wonder what ever made you come to New York? He's the answer.

It is comfortable and comforting to know what you know. You know your home town and the people there. Girls like Becky. You see visions of high school— the dances, the football games, study hall, and the prom. The spaghetti dinner at San Bartolomeo's. Snipe hunting at the beach.

And you know HIM. You know the whims, the fun, the hopes, the passions. With him something could happen—you know—just like back then. Maybe. Minus the adrenaline rush.

TEEN CRUSH (NOW)

TRAINWRECK

How He Expresses His Interests

"With kids in college and alimony payments, I can barely make my greens fees."

"Remember when I ran your department? Made sure we took customers to Michelin 3-Star restaurants. And we all flew business class."

"What kind of vermouth do you have?"

How He Presents His Accomplishments

"For 5 years straight in the '90s we were the top performers in the industry."

"I've been through it all. Slipped disk. Knee surgery. Bypass. Gout."

"My second wife expected me to become CEO. She's beautiful, and younger than you. Too bad she left me."

"I can't believe they chose that half-load for CEO. They could have had me!"

How He Tells You He Likes You

"My shrink thinks we should go out—be good for me."

"How much does someone at your level make these days?"

"Will you get a pension or just a 401k?"

"I don't have health insurance."

How He Asks You to Bed

"I'm depressed tonight."

"I need help with my Social Security enrollment forms."

How He Talks About Your Future Together

"My ex-girlfriend was great in bed. But then she got married."

"Think I'll move to Greensboro. Be near my folks. And the golf courses are better."

"My ex-girlfriend called me last night. We spoke for 2 hours. I thought that you should know. We should be brutally honest with each other."

"I told my daughter that I'd support her for a few years after drama school."

Why You Should Date Him

Why not go out to the best places in town, with a guy who is sharp, witty, worldly, well dressed, sophisticated, handsome, and confident? A guy who's made it to upper management at least once, with amusing war stories to prove it? Your friends and colleagues will approve. Some of them may even have heard of him. So what if he's a little bit older, wobbly, and perennially out of work? So what if you pay the tab? Who cares? He's available! And he never complains when you ask him to escort you to your business dinners. Provided they have the right vermouth.

When you are sentenced to serve as a bridesmaid for the second or third time, you might ask yourself, "Why don't I get married like everyone else? Am I too picky? So what if these guys aren't perfect?"

After all, how bad could marriage to one of them be?

JACK OF HEARTS

Being good will be a charming novelty for Jack. Jack may settle down and play faithful husband long enough to have kids. After a few years of wrenching abstinence, he will find himself at a charity ball or some such, drink too much, and fall into the arms of the hostess, the hat-check girl, or a bar maid. This newfound earth-moving passion will be the first of many to come.

BOY WONDER

Despite his current living situation—the low-rent apartment with two roommates from college—Boy Wonder knows that his future life is a mansion on Long Island Sound with three cars, two kids, and a super-model wife. So if you are not Giselle Bundschen, you've got to have a lot of money and/or influential relatives and business contacts. Boy Wonder will start out as an impeccable husband and father. After all, he's worked his whole life to deserve your money, relatives, and contacts. But when he gets passed up for promotion, he won't be coming to you for comfort. First stop: Tanqueray. Second stop: the size-6 office administrator from Ronkonkoma.

BORN AGAIN BACHELOR

After your marriage, the bulk of his income will go to the upkeep of the Lamborghini and the other personal toys. The remainder will go to his ex-wife and ex-kids in New Jersey. This means that your income will go to the new house and the new kids. After about 4 years, he'll renew his search for the ultimate woman. He'll get a studio apartment on the Upper East Side, where he is closer to more of the women he meets on the internet. You'll know that his years with you did him some good if he dates a woman over 30. From time to time, he'll want to bring some of his candidates out to meet the kids. It will count as quality time.

DIALTONE

You won't have to spend thousands on sleep aids, Jacuzzis, chiropractors, or chocolate to wind down. You'll have your own personal white noise machine. But as Dialtone's wife, you'll also be facing solitary for 30 years to life. Just like in one of his beloved Law and Order re-runs.

CLOUD VOYAGER

You'll have the marriage that your mother wanted: you will have complete control. You will decide where to live, what house to buy, how many kids to have, and where they'll attend school. None of these things will interest Cloud Voyager because they aren't happening on the Ho Chi Minh trail. When he finds nothing exotic on the commuter train from Patchogue, he will become existentially bored and then despondent. Unless you want to sign up for an irrigation project in Nepal or run a B&B in Botswana, Cloud Voyager isn't the man for you.

DON JUAN DINERO

Don Juan Dinero will marry a 16-year-old Argentine virgin who has never left her family's compound. You probably don't qualify, fortunately for you. Otherwise, you'd be stuck on a large estate in Asuncion, La Paz, or Padua. His extended family would also be there. They would ignore you. If you looked at another man, you'd be shot.

CLUB CADET

You'll spend your engagement touring every house for sale in suburban Connecticut. When you're married, he'll make constructive comments on how to improve your wardrobe, cooking, muscle tone, and hairstyle. Frequently. He'll do so with the help of visual aids from Town and Country, Vogue, and the Saks Fifth Avenue catalog. You might as well go live with your mother.

HOPALONG HUSBAND

Hopalong is passionate about you because he is not risking a commitment to you. In his reasoning, he is already committed to Doris. And look how that turned out.

VISIONARY

Your marriage will last as long as his art fails. Somebody needs to support him. So you could be together for very a long time—probably forever. After you're married, you will no longer be invited to meet his friends at the pub or go to gallery openings. That's because you are no longer a friend. You're his wife. If you were a friend, you would have paid for everything without getting married.

TREADMILL

You will see him only on weekends and legal holidays when the office is closed. During those times he will be working in your den, surfacing only for meals or attending one of the kids' soccer games. At dinner, he will keep his smartphone next to his plate so he can read his emails in real time. He'll take business calls in bed. With round-the-clock telecommunications, sex will be short, when it happens. Every 2 or 3 years, you'll have to pack up and move to some awful city—Riyadh, Djakarta, El Paso—where the company has an outpost. He will spend all of his waking time on alert at the outpost.

MAJOR GELATIN

He won't marry you until he's divorced. So if his wife decides to stay with him, it's over. It's also over if she decides to divorce. That's because the divorce will take 10 to 15 years to work its way through court as he and his wife struggle over each asset. He won't be able to see you during the case because his wife's team is tracking his every move, and he'll be slapped with yet another charge of adultery. All you'll have to show for the many years you've devoted to him will be anonymous love poems in the mail and unsigned postcards from places like Cape Horn and the South China Sea where he's on his boat and, no doubt, still thinking of you.

TEEN CRUSH

Your mother expects you to visit her at least twice a week. Becky barges into your hubby's tiny apartment with no warning. You can't find a job, and there is nothing to do except bingo at San Bartolomeo's. Your new husband Crush does exactly the same thing every day. The smallest change—like booking a matinee movie when he's scheduled to mow the lawn—generates panic, as does putting a salad bowl in a different cupboard. You'll remember how you felt about your home town the first time you lived there: "I'm so bored I could spit."

TRAINWRECK

You will have to tell your financial planner to add another 10 years to your projected retirement date. You'll need to keep your company's spousal health benefits and fund your step-daughter while she auditions. After an exhausting day at work, you'll come home to find Train Wreck relaxing in front of the TV with a Bombay gin martini and waiting impatiently for you to make dinner. While he's playing golf on Saturday, he'll expect you to represent the family at an Off-Off-Broadway matinee of Mother Courage in which his daughter performs as an extra.

You deserve better and you already have better. You make a good living, and have a comfortable apartment. Your wide circle of friends and your interests keep your social calendar full. You can go anywhere in the world at the drop of a hat, and be able to stay at a 4-star hotel or with friends. Why would you let marriage ruin your life?

You won't, unless, of course, you meet Mr. Right.

MR. RIGHT

How He Expresses His Interests

"Your knowledge of Japan is truly remarkable. I can think of nothing more exciting than having you join me on my next trip there in April."

"I am just learning to paint, but I would, in any event, like to immortalize your features on canvas. By any chance, would you sit for me?"

"My boat is a terrible extravagance, and I really should dispense with it, but if that's what it takes for me to see you in a bikini, why I shall simply have to outfit it once again for St. George."

"The mayor was convinced that Tom Hanks wouldn't come to my fundraiser, but we proved him wrong. I'm sure they found me a poor host, though. I was so entranced by your stories of life in corporate America that I hardly had a chance to talk to either of them."

"Perhaps my greatest satisfaction derives from being a Big Brother to two kids in the South Bronx. Those kids really need a man to talk to. It's made me realize how much I'll enjoy [looking at you] being a parent."

How He Presents His Accomplishments

"Don't listen to Father. I simply was not the youngest editor in the history of the Harvard Law Review. Every time I come home to Petherton, they come up with another extravagant and entirely undeserved tribute. The only tribute I deserve is for making you mine."

"I must admit that over the last several months my thinking of you has all but ended my external pursuits. My translations of Pindar and my hieroglyph poetry have gone unattended. But I don't regret it at all."

"I learned to make sushi when I came back to the States. I shall perfect it since you enjoy it so much."

How He Tells You He Likes You

"You are unlike any woman I've ever known."

"You are so lovely, intelligent, and witty and yet so remarkably tender."

"It seems as though we've always known each other. We're so at ease and compatible. I must have been a saint in my previous life."

"I'd like you to meet my mother when she visits town."

"Let's ignore the Super Bowl. I'd rather shop for rings at Cartier."

"What beautiful children you'll have."

How He Asks You to Bed

He will know when you want to become intimate. It will happen after enough time has gone by that you won't appear too hasty, but before you begin to doubt his interest.

"I love you."

"Please marry me."

"You don't need to lose weight."

How He Talks About Your Future Together

He will propose on the ninth or tenth date, or after you've known each other for 4 or 5 weeks. As he'll tell you, he couldn't wait any longer.

Why You Should Date Him

Why wouldn't you? He is head-over-heels in love with you.

It will be a wedding to remember.

There will be no pre-nup.

9 781946 300560